Walking with Pain
The Lonely Journey

John Elliston

WALKING WITH PAIN
The Lonely Journey

Copyright © 2005 John P. Elliston
Original edition published in English under the title WALKING
WITH PAIN by Kevin Mayhew Ltd, Buxhall, England.
This edition copyright © Fortress Press 2019

All rights reserved. Except for brief quotations in critical articles
or reviews, no part of this book may be reproduced in any
manner without prior written permission from the publisher.
Email copyright@augsburgfortress.org or write to Permissions,
Fortress Press, PO Box 1209, Minneapolis, MN 55440-1209.

Scripture quotations are from *The Revised Standard Version of the
Bible*, copyright © 1946, 1952 and 1971 by the Division of Christian
Education of the National Council of Churches in the USA. Used
by permission.

Cover image: Photo by Daniel Leone on Unsplash
Cover design: Joe Reinke

Print ISBN: 978-1-5064-5971-4

CONTENTS

	About the Author	4
	Preface	5
	Introduction	7
1.	So Full of Pain	9
2.	A Black Hole	11
3.	Nothing but Pain	13
4.	Strength Cut Away	15
5.	Consider the Ravens	17
6.	Life Goes On	19
7.	Mortality	21
8.	No Exit	23
9.	Carry Me, This Way	25
10.	The Island of Pain	27
11.	The Touch that Heals	29
12.	The Way of Emptiness	31
13.	So Much Love	33
14.	Everything You Need to Know	35
15.	Do Not Be Afraid	37
16.	They Will Watch over You	39
17.	Divine Leading	41
18.	Mercifully, There Are Times of Sleep	43
19.	"I and My Father Are One"	45

About the Author

The Reverend Dr. John Elliston is a Baptist minister, currently working at Grange Road Baptist Church in Darlington, England. He has written a number of books of prayers including *Here in Our Midst*, *Footprints on Sand*, *From the Depths*, *From the Foot of the Cross,* and *Walking the Way of the Cross: Prayers For Your Personal Journey*.

Preface

Pain is inseparable from the human condition, defining our humanity. Mercifully, for most, it comes into life as an infrequent guest. For some, however, it becomes a constant companion with whom an unequal battle is fought. In this particular publication, the author explores the phenomenon of pain through pain experienced, and places the whole into the context of belief in a loving God.

*Spirit of Christ,
enlarge my vision,
calm my heart,
and walk with me as I travel
the dark and lonely road of pain.*

Introduction

From the beginning Christian theologians have grappled with the existence of pain; indeed, Christianity, with its central symbol of the cross, means there is a certain inevitability in this engagement. For the most part their energies have been sublimated into the larger question of the problem of evil, addressing questions like how the existence of pain can be reconciled with a belief in a good and loving God. Such studies have offered many profound and valuable insights which enable people to live with pain in a meaningful way. In what follows, however, I have deliberately avoided engaging with pain at this level, but have concentrated on those points where pain is raw, where it is less about intellectual struggle and more about the emotions. Where pain is raw, it is not theology that fills the mind, but disbelief, grief, doubt, anger. Why me? Why now? It is loss, it is denial, it is wanting to escape, it is meaninglessness, it is not wanting to wake up, it is wanting to die.

1
So Full of Pain

> My world, so full of pain, is placed in a world
> where everything is normal.

Lord, I left no place at the table of my life for pain,
no room for its abiding,
no provision for its voracious appetite.
And yet it has come, pushing aside invited guests—
my dreams, my hopes, my loves—
demanding time and space, that I had reserved for
 better, more creative things.

Beyond, I see another world,
a world without shadows
where people move unhindered,
undistracted by the inner voice
that with every unplanned movement
becomes a scream,
and which turns every summer's day to winter.

"I just want to be normal," my body shouts,
but no one hears . . . because there is no one to hear;
a stranded yachtsman adrift on the lonely ocean of
 pain,
tossed between rage and panic,
between hope and despair,

by unrelenting waves that batter my fragile body
until I can take no more,
and every heartbeat longing for rescue.

Lord, you have known pain;

the pain of nails piercing your flesh,
and the deeper pain of facing it alone,
without a Father's love.

Speak your word against the raging storm
and as once on a Galilean sea,
restore the calm and grant your peace.

Amen.

2

A Black Hole

Lord, I am cast into turmoil,
emotionally in free-fall.
Pain has swept the solid ground from beneath me,
and I am tumbling into a darkness
unknown and unborn,
a strange world in which I am a stranger to myself
and where everything is unfamiliar.
I am as a refugee, abandoned in an alien land,
distant in place, distant in language,
where, as adept as I am with words,
I am the foreigner not understood.

Lord, do you understand
the coded screams behind "Yes, I'm fine,"
the silences filled with fear,
and the darkness that threatens to swallow me
  whole?

How fragile
are the pedestals on which we stand,
the certainties
upon which we build our tomorrows,
the vain calculation of the years, "I am too young,"
the furtive glances toward the pain of others,
the belief that goodness offers some kind of immunity!

John Elliston

But in a single moment of pain,
their careful logic is broken,
and the fall begins . . .
at first there is struggle to hold on to what was,
to stand upon yesterday's certainty,
but gravity is a powerful adversary
and I am helpless
before this silent and aggressive foe.

Lord, as I fall into the darkness of pain
and descend into the despair
of the abandoned and the alone,
help me to believe that my fall will be broken by
   love
and that, beneath me, are your ever-loving arms.

Amen.

3

Nothing but Pain

Lord, there is nothing but pain;
it fills every moment.
I want to escape.
I am like a child lost in a maze,
searching for the exit that will bring me back
to the world I have left behind—

the predictable world, where there are no
   dead ends;
the safe world, where I am in control;
the yesterday world, where there is no pain.

But there is no escape.

Pain on my left side,
pain on my right side,
pain before me,
pain behind me,

its sharp barbs pierce my body like the thorns of a
redeemer's crown
and in my despair I cry—

"My God, my God, why have you forsaken me?"
Occasionally, the memory of another time

fills my mind—
of running across an open field,
the wind rushing through my hair
and every muscle answering in joy,
of dancing among the rock falls of laughter,
of hope, and of freedom
that anticipates tomorrow.
But even memory is painful now.
It taunts me with regret for what I have wasted,
while resentment tortures my mind
with what might have been.

Lord, help me to value what I have,
to greet every new day as a divine gift,
and to try to live in moments rather than lifespans.

Amen.

4

Strength Cut Away

When Deli'lah saw that he had told her all his mind, she sent and called the lords of the Philistines, saying, "Come up this once, for he has told me all his mind." Then the lords of the Philistines came up to her, and brought the money in their hands. She made him sleep upon her knees; and she called a man, and had him shave off the seven locks of his head. Then she began to torment him, and his strength left him.

Judges 16:18–19

Lord, I believed it could never happen to me—
my strength, like Samson's was unassailable,

my stamina endless,
and my energy a well that was never dry.

But pain has robbed me,
my body is self-betrayed,
and the friend upon whom I had placed so much
  reliance
has become the all-consuming enemy.

Each day is a burden now,
moving endlessly through the things that have to
  be done,

John Elliston

those things upon which survival depends—

eating, washing, dressing.

While imagination brims with what could be done,

the battles to be fought,
the mountains to be climbed,
the dreams yet to be fulfilled.

But the grip of pain is unyielding,
paralyzing the body within the world of what is,
and consigning to dust what could have been.

Lord, my helplessness torments me
as if I were somehow responsible,
somehow to blame,
but my hands are stretched out by another
and it is pain that carries me where I have no wish
   to go.

On this lonely journey,
grant me the courage to resist the inner torment,
the wisdom not to surrender to self-doubt,
and the faith to believe that, within,
you are the resources to endure this
   unimagined situation.

Amen.

5

Consider the Ravens

> *"Consider the ravens: they neither sow nor reap, they have neither storehouse nor barn, and yet God feeds them. Of how much more value are you than the birds!"* Luke 12:24

Lord, you speak of the value of the raven,
yet everything that has given me worth and value
has been stolen by pain,
even my trust in you—
have I done something wrong in the past?
In the far reaches of yesterday,
has some unforgivable sin scarred the cells of my body
and turned them to violence?
Did you speak of ravens because the raven never sings?

Lord, let me hear birdsong again.
Let it come to me as fresh and clear
as when a blackbird spoke for the first time,
and filled creation with a sound so beautiful
that the mountains trembled
and the streams of the mountains erupted in applause.

John Elliston

May I not become so fearful of pain
that it prevents me finding pleasure
in the pleasurable moments of life—

in the warmth of a summer sun,
in the beauty of nature,
in loving friends who give me time.

And may I find within them
a meaning that fills the empty coffers of my heart.

Lord, I feel as nothing,
help me to believe that the "nothingness" is of you,
and that in experiencing its darkness
I may, in some mysterious way, find you,
and so hear the raven sing.

Amen.

6

Life Goes On

Lord, life goes on, but I am removed from it.
Pain is its own world, with its own language—
palliative care, diversion, cognitive therapy—
while the ordinary world remains as distant as a
dream . . . so near and yet so far.
Desperation tries to bridge the gap—
acupuncture, antidepressant, analgesic—
hopes rise,
and I, like an asylum seeker boarding a train,
hoping against hope that this time
the guardians of that other world
will not notice me as I slip through.

Life goes on, but it does not mean what it used to
 mean;
pain has robbed me of its joy.
Energy is spent in survival,
in passing from one moment to the next,
leaving time for nothing
except the demands of my own wretched body
and for the fear that with the next wave
I will be totally overwhelmed.

Lord, save me from becoming so self-absorbed
that I have no time for the people around me.

Grant me the grace to feel tenderness and sympathy
   for others,
to acknowledge that, in this often cruel world,
I have no monopoly on pain,
that others are hurting too,
and so not to impose upon them the burden that,
ultimately, I alone must carry.
Though pain has robbed me of what was,
help me to believe that life does, indeed, go on.

Amen.

7

Mortality

For while we live we are always being given up to death for Jesus' sake, so that the life of Jesus may be manifested in our mortal flesh. So death is at work in us, but life in you.

2 Corinthians 4:11–12

Lord, this life that we share is a transient gift;
we carry its seed within us across the years,
finding joy and knowing sadness,
experiencing laughter and shedding tears,
but we know it is not forever
and that every breath we take
is a footstep toward the day of our departing.

We have been created mortal;
to be human is to be living and dying at the same time,
to be suspended upon a fragile strand,
precariously balanced,
as on a tightrope,
somewhere between a beginning and an end.

Lord, pain sharpens my sense of mortality,
strips back the pretence of invulnerability,
seeds my mind with the fear of losing all that I value,
exposes me to forces that will bring me to my end.

John Elliston

I am full of apprehension;
frightened that death will catch me unawares,
frightened of oblivion,
frightened of the stories that I will leave unfinished.

Lord, grant me courage as I move toward tomorrow,
so that I may write love's signature upon this
   human pilgrimage
and, in the ultimate surrender that I know must come,
believe that all is a surrender to you.

Amen.

8
No Exit

Lord, the sun lies on the other side;
an impenetrable wall of pain and fear blocks its light
and I grope in darkness to find a way through.
Occasionally, the brightness surprises,
like opening a door on a summer's day
and being momentarily blinded
(thank you for the good days).
But for the most part the sun is on the other side,
and the door is clearly marked "no exit."

How desperately I want to leave this wood,
to join the ranks of those whose lives,
free from the constraints of pain,
are locked into uncritical normality—

hurrying to the next appointment,
standing in conversation with a friend,
waiting for the bus that will probably never come.

But life is not normal;
pain has carried me out of the mainstream of life
and marooned me here—
alone, engulfed, and overwhelmed.

Lord, you are present in the dark wood of pain,
when its uncertain paths lead to confusion

and when its cruel intensity threatens
to snuff out all life's joys.
Above all, Father of the forsaken Christ,
you are there when I feel forsaken,
opening my heart to the suffering of others,
deepening my empathy
and helping me to understand that,
even in this God-forsaken place,
I am not alone.

Amen.

9

Carry Me, This Way

Lord, pain is a harsh and austere teacher;
its lessons are wrought in places and times
that are unchosen
and into which most journey unprepared.
It's an enforced way
along which suffering humanity travels alone.

It is said that pain can purify,
ennoble, bring us to our senses,
that it can offer new insight and help wisdom to
  grow.
But it can also brutalize, humiliate, and destroy;
it can take away dignity,
and carry us to places
that are far from where we desire to go . . .

away from all that is familiar,
all that is loved, and all that is dreamt of.

And yet,
even in the presence of such an austere teacher,
there are still choices to be made;
every day, every hour, every moment,
there are opportunities to choose—
between hope and despair,

between faith and fatalism,
between resistance and surrender.

And with every choice the power to direct its path
in ways that do not diminish the human,
but affirm it.

Lord, there are many aspects of pain that are
  beyond my control,
but my attitude is not one of them.
Deliver me from resentment,
from anger,
from a gnawing jealousy that strikes the people I
  love.
Deliver me from the temptation to become less
  than I am,
so that in the choices I make,
I may become greater.

Amen.

10

The Island of Pain

Lord, my pain is a small space,
it is an island in a slowly rising sea;
the incoming tide erodes my fragile defenses,
and the smaller the island becomes,
the less I have, the less I want, the less I need,
as if my wanting is diminished by the space
that remains for me to be me.

Yesterday, I set store by possessions,

the size of my bank account,
the expanding horizons of ambition,
the latest gadget, too complicated to use,

and with every fiber of my being
I have fought to hold back the encroaching tide,
even to regain the ground, that pain had taken
 from me—
but to no avail.
Today, I don't even give thought to what I had,
I just want to stay at the same level,
to not hurt any more.

I am so tired of fighting,
tired of having to make an effort
in a world that others can negotiate so effortlessly,

John Elliston

tired of the same daily routine in a world that seems,
by the minute,
to be getting smaller.

Lord, I belong to the island of pain.
It tells me who I am
when everything else has been taken away,
it is the one place over which I have some control.
And it gives the visitor somewhere to come,
bearing the only gift that really matters—their love.

Amen.

11

The Touch that Heals

Lord, my body is no longer my own;
I am a disease that doctors examine,
I am a pathology that seeks a cure,
I am a number on a wristband that has no name—
an object in a medical world in which I am a stranger,
even to myself.

Daily they come,
white-robed priests drawing from my veins
a story acted out upon a larger human stage—
red cells, white cells, hemoglobin—
examining the cells of my body
  as if they were not me—
but they are me, because without them I would not be.

Lord, touch me with the palm of your hand,
flesh on flesh;
let me feel the warm embrace of human compassion,
the gentle whisper of divine love;
for I need to know that this body is still my body,
that the disease and pain which have invaded me
have not finally triumphed,
that inside the shell,
assaulted by knife, by needle, and the liturgy of cure,
there is me, vulnerable, afraid, and needing your love.

John Elliston

Lord, touch me and make me whole—

touch me with the hand of my beloved,
touch me with a child's hand,
touch me with the hand of a stranger,

for, paradoxically, I know
that every human touch is a touch that heals.

Amen.

12

The Way of Emptiness

And though the Lord give you the bread of adversity and the water of affliction, yet your Teacher will not hide himself any more, but your eyes shall see your Teacher. And your ears shall hear a word behind you, saying, "This is the way, walk in it," when you turn to the right or when you turn to the left. Then you will defile your silver-covered graven images and your gold-plated molten images. You will scatter them as unclean things; you will say to them, "Begone!"

Isaiah 30:20–22

Lord, there is a kenosis call in pain—
it strips bear the trappings
with which we usually dress up our humanity,
it disfigures and distorts the body
and takes away the defenses behind which we hide.
Naked we came into the world,
and naked we shall depart from it.*

Lord, when everything is taken away, what is left?
Do I become a nonperson, an outcast,

---

* Job 1:21: "Naked I came from my mother's womb, and naked shall I return . . ."

an object in other people's worlds?
Or do love, and hope, and faith
survive to tell the story which is me?

It is in the emptiness of pain
that I have learned what really matters,
that love is the most precious of gifts,
that people matter more than things,
and wholeness is to be found,
not among the gods of independence and
   self-reliance
but in the humility that is content to be carried,
and in the life that finds fulfillment in you.

Amen.

13

So Much Love

Lord, I am loved;
I am loved more than I could ever have realized
before pain gave me the eyes to see—
the gentle hand that comforts me,
adding its strength to mine when all my resources
 are gone,
the loving eyes that show the warmth of
understanding, when I feel so alone,
and the voices that speak peace and compassion to
 my tortured soul.

Thank you for the love that surrounds me;
for a healing power capable of directing the stars,
but which comes to me in ordinary ways;
through the cards and letters that tumble through
 the door,
through the meal so lovingly prepared
and the visits, short and long, full of voices and silence,
that assure me I am not forgotten.

Lord, help me to be open to the lives of those
 around me;
help me not to become so absorbed by my own
 inner agonies
that I have no compassion for, or worse, fail to notice,
the pain of others.

John Elliston

Grant me the grace to see,
as you saw from the cross,
the pain of your mother and your dearest friend,
and there to choose the way of love,
rather than impose upon those closest to me
the somber injustices of my own crucifixion.

Amen.

14

Everything You Need to Know

> There are things we know that we don't know
> that we know, until we need them . . .

Lord, my body cries out in pain;
there is a cold silence that casts a shadow over
   what I was.
I yearn for yesterday's joys,
for the freedom of a life
that is not bounded by limitation—

no longer captive to a body
that will not answer the call to run,
and dance, and move freely
in the world that you have given,

no longer the prisoner of forces that I cannot control,
no longer the cared for,
but the one who controls my every tomorrow.

I am no longer my own.

And yet, from somewhere within me,
there is a strength that I do not recognize,
resources of which I was unaware,

John Elliston

an inner power,
that has enabled me to face
what I never believed I could.

Is it you?

The unseen hand that guides my path,
the comforting touch that stills my tortured mind,
the hand on my shoulder that says "be strong."

Lord, on this journey,

I have discovered more of myself than I knew before,

the unfathomable depths of human fear,
a capacity to face what I never believed I could,
my inner poverty and my total reliance on you.

I did not choose to come this way,
but I am grateful I have.

Amen.

15

Do Not Be Afraid

Lord, from the day that pain entered my life,
there was fear;
some of it rational, understandable,
based upon what is happening to me—

the fear of losing control,
the fear of being unable to cope,
the fear of the assault on my body becoming worse.

Far deeper, however, is the irrational fear,
   cold and alien;

a band of steel around my stomach
a reservoir of dread inside my soul
an inner journey through inexplicable torment.

It is said that perfect love casts out fear—
that love bears the fearful upon angels' wings
to find new freedom,
not by escaping or eliminating fear,
but by transcending it . . .
acknowledging its presence,
but refusing it permission to speak the last word.

John Elliston

Lord, you love me;
you do not need to be persuaded to enter the place
　of fear,
you walk beside me within it
as surely as you walked with Christ to the Cross,
and even though the path is dark,
you do not leave me to face it alone.
In the night of fear, grant me the courage to trust
　you,

to surrender my journey into your unseen hand,
to let you lead me through the valley of shadow,
to tread where you have trod and so to
　follow your way,

for you are the God who redeems me,
and yours is the love that says, "Be not afraid."

Amen.

16

They Will Watch over You

When you walk, they will lead you; when you lie down, they will watch over you; and when you awake, they will talk with you.
Proverbs 6:22

Lord, the anatomy of pain is anonymous.
It moves within me,
violently twisting my body into its own likeness—

the sudden flexing of uncontrolled limbs,
the anger that erupts as illness,
the sense of being self-betrayed.

Anonymous, too, is the providence that guides me,
the unseen force that is greater than pain,
that moves all creation
to a destiny that lives within you,
and which gives a purpose
even to that which disfigures and destroys.

And yet, in Christ, providence has a human shape,
it is a voice that guides,
it is a hand that holds,
it is a presence
that accompanies me through the darkness.

John Elliston

And sometimes providence loses its anonymity,
it is a colleague whose wise counsel
helps me cope with the emotions that pain evokes,
it is a lover who sits and watches through the night
so that even in sleep I am not alone,
it is a friend whose conversation assures me
that limited as it is, my life still matters.

Lord, what happens to me belongs to you—
"You lead me beside still waters . . . "
And even though I walk through the valley of death,
you calm me.
When pain weighs me down
and anxiety casts a shadow over your love,
teach me that my fear is only the fear of being
   afraid.

Amen.

17
Divine Leading

Lord, I don't know how it will end.
Each day, more pain,
and tomorrow, and tomorrow . . .
Each day a little more frightened,
my body a little more diminished.

The stream of life carries me relentlessly forward—

into a future that I have not chosen,
into a destiny for which I am unprepared.

Once I dreamed of success,
of good reputation,
of achievement.
Today there is nothing but the pain—

casting its shadow on every hope,
destroying every dream,
demanding my every resource;

it feels as if I am just hanging on.
Lord, grant me the faith to believe
that the stream on which I am borne
  is your providence.
Sustain me with a sense of life's continuity
and grant me the courage to say that life is good,

even though it trickles through my fingers
and evades my every attempt to hold it.
In the uncertainty of tomorrow,
may I have the grace to be thankful for
   the gift of today
and may the unremitting current of time
carry me gently into the ocean of your love.

Amen.

18

Mercifully, There Are Times of Sleep

Lord, thank you for the gift of sleep,
time out from the thought of pain,
an escape wherein, for brief moments,
I can believe that this isn't happening to me.

In my dreams there is no pain,
transitory though it is, I sink into myself,
finding within the womb of unconscious imagination
a home for my brokenness.
Asleep, I am no different from anyone else,
dead to the world and to myself.

Lord, there is healing in sleep,
a tactical withdrawal of the body that enables my
  resources to be regathered and hope to be reborn,
the promise of a new tomorrow,
a surrender to darkness
that summons the light of a new dawn.
And yet in sleep I am vulnerable, exposed,
  and unguarded.
Watch over me as I sleep,
embrace my dreams within your peace
and my fears within your silence

that, held in the outstretched arms of the Calvary
   Christ,
my soul may be safe.

Lord, the healing gift of sleep
anticipates the final healing that will come as death,
when, like shedding the cares of the day,
I will shed this worn-out body
that has been both enemy and friend,
and all things will be made new in you.
"Into your hands I commend my spirit."

Amen.

19

"I and My Father Are One"

Lord, however weak and frail I may become,
my body remains interconnected with all that exists;
in you I live and move and have my being.

From the beginning you have known me,
you formed the innermost parts of my being,
and before ever I had breath, you embraced me,
as you embrace me now,
wrapping me in your compassion,
healing my brokenness,
restoring my soul.

Lord, I am safe within your love.
The waters are calm,
and the gentle moonlight bathes my tortured soul.
Nothing can touch me now;
the pain is gone,
and everything that once screamed within me,
that crucified my body and tortured my mind,
has passed, like the night before the breaking day.

Let me sleep now,
let me dream within the peace that is beyond
  understanding—

the peace of a child sucking at its mother's breast,
the peace of a lover in the arms of the beloved,
the peace a prodigal finally coming home.

May I know, finally and absolutely,
that nothing can take me from the security of
   this place.
That we are one.
And that pain will never again sunder our union.

Amen.

www.ingramcontent.com/pod-product-compliance
Lightning Source LLC
Chambersburg PA
CBHW052037070526
44584CB00020B/3143